Flying Deep

Climb Inside Deep-Sea Submersible ALVIN

Michelle Cusolito

Illustrated by Nicole Wong

Charlesbridge

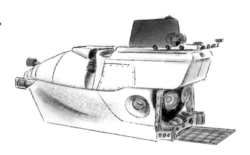

To Rick, my adventure-loving husband and my biggest supporter.
I couldn't have done it without you.
        —M. C.

To Dan.
        —N. W.

Special thanks to Don Collasius, former *Alvin* pilot, for hours of interviews and for reading an early draft; to Joanne Tromp, information officer at Woods Hole Oceanographic Institution, for providing resources and connecting me to Bruce Strickrott, manager of the Alvin Group; and most important, to Bruce, for his incredible support throughout the writing of this book and for vetting the final text and art.—M. C.

Published by Charlesbridge
85 Main Street
Watertown, MA 02472
(617) 926-0329
www.charlesbridge.com

Library of Congress Cataloging-in-Publication Data
Names: Cusolito, Michelle, author. | Wong, Nicole (Nicole E.), illustrator.
Title: Flying deep: [climb inside deep-sea submersible Alvin] / Michelle Cusolito; illustrated by [Nicole Wong].
Description: Watertown, Massachusetts: Charlesbridge, [2018] | Includes bibliographical references and index.
Identifiers: LCCN 2017012925 (print) | LCCN 2017039444 (ebook) | ISBN 9781632896568 (ebook)
| ISBN 9781632896575 (ebook pdf) | ISBN 9781580898119 (reinforced for library use: alk. paper)
| ISBN 9781580898416 (softcover)
Subjects: LCSH: Oceanographic submersibles—Massachusetts—Woods Hole—Juvenile literature.
| Underwater exploration—Juvenile literature.
Classification: LCC GC67 (ebook) | LCC GC67 .C87 2018 (print) | DDC 627/.704—dc23
LC record available at https://lccn.loc.gov/2017012925

Printed in China
(hc) 10 9 8 7 6 5 4 3 2
(sc) 10 9 8 7 6 5 4 3 2 1

Illustrations created digitally on the iPad using the Procreate app
Display type set in Rabbits by Typetype
Text type set in Mikado by Hannes von Doehren
Color separations by Colourscan Print Co Pte Ltd, Singapore
Printed by 1010 Printing International Limited in Huizhou, Guangdong, China
Production supervision by Brian G. Walker
Designed by Diane M. Earley

Imagine
you're the pilot
of *Alvin*,
a deep-sea submersible
barely big enough for three.

Today you'll investigate
the site of deadly explosions.
Many years ago
underwater volcanoes
erupted.
Red-hot lava
blasted
from deep inside Earth.
An ecosystem was destroyed.

Remarkably, life returned
again and again.

Your mission:
Survey the site,
confirm thriving life,
and collect specimens.

What will you discover?

Lower yourself
through *Alvin*'s hatch.
Flip on oxygen—
pssssssssssss.
Switch on carbon dioxide scrubber—
zzzzzzzzhhhhhhhh.

Two scientists
squeeze between gear.
You stand and seal the sphere,
silencing the world outside.
Call *Atlantis*: "HATCH IS SHUT."

Launch coordinator asks captain,
"PERMISSION TO LAUNCH?"
"CLEARED TO LAUNCH."
Alvin shudders gently when boomed out
and lowered into the Pacific—
splash!

Swimmers inspect *Alvin*'s exterior.
Surface controller calls,
"FREE OF SHIP."
Atlantis motors away.

Perform final checks.
"PERMISSION TO DIVE?"
"GRANTED. SWIMMERS CLEAR."

8:00 a.m.
Alvin
sinks,
slowly spinning

DOWN DOWN DOWN.

Your stomach flutters.

Clear water becomes aqua.

DOWN DOWN DOWN.

Breathe slowly and easily.
There's enough oxygen.

We pilots choose music
for the long journey
into the abyss.
Will you choose
calming classical?
Energizing hip-hop?

Aqua becomes blue-green.

DOWN DOWN DOWN.

Analyze ocean currents.
Monitor the speed of descent
to determine your exact location.

Enter thick blackness.
Constellations
of alien-like animals
twinkle and glow.
A natural fireworks show.
Do you look as foreign to them
as they look to you?

9:00 a.m.

As *Alvin* descends,
temperatures drop.
Pull on a sweatshirt and hat.

Sonar sounds—
ping, ping
pop
    tink
pop
    tink.

Nearly two miles deep,
you've reached the seafloor.
Release starboard weight—
click, shhhhh.
Alvin rolls slightly.

You only see
what's in your beam of light.
Inch the joystick forward to glide ahead.
Whirring thrusters churn
silt and mud
and bits of dead organisms
as you fly along the murky bottom.

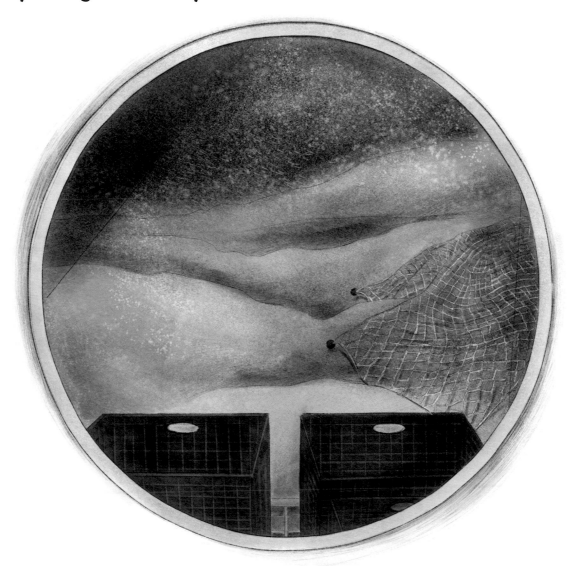

Watch out!
Fishing nets or anchor chains
could entangle *Alvin*
and trap you.

10:00 a.m.

A desolate landscape stretches before you.
Soar along
sloping mounds
of cooled lava.
Like a puppeteer,
use the miniature arm inside
to control the large arm outside.
Grasp a piece of glassy rock.
Drop it into the sample basket.

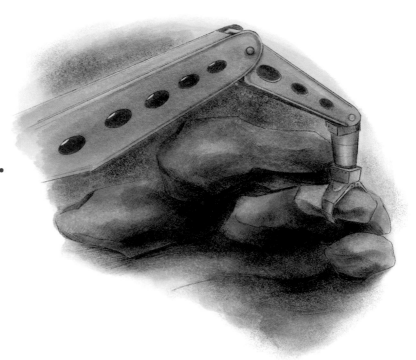

Movement
out the starboard porthole
catches your eye.
A ghost crab!
Could there be more?

Fly forward.
Watch for jutting vent chimneys
as you tunnel through darkness.

Eerie spires loom.
Black smokers blast
scalding water
and poisonous, sooty particles
from deep inside Earth.

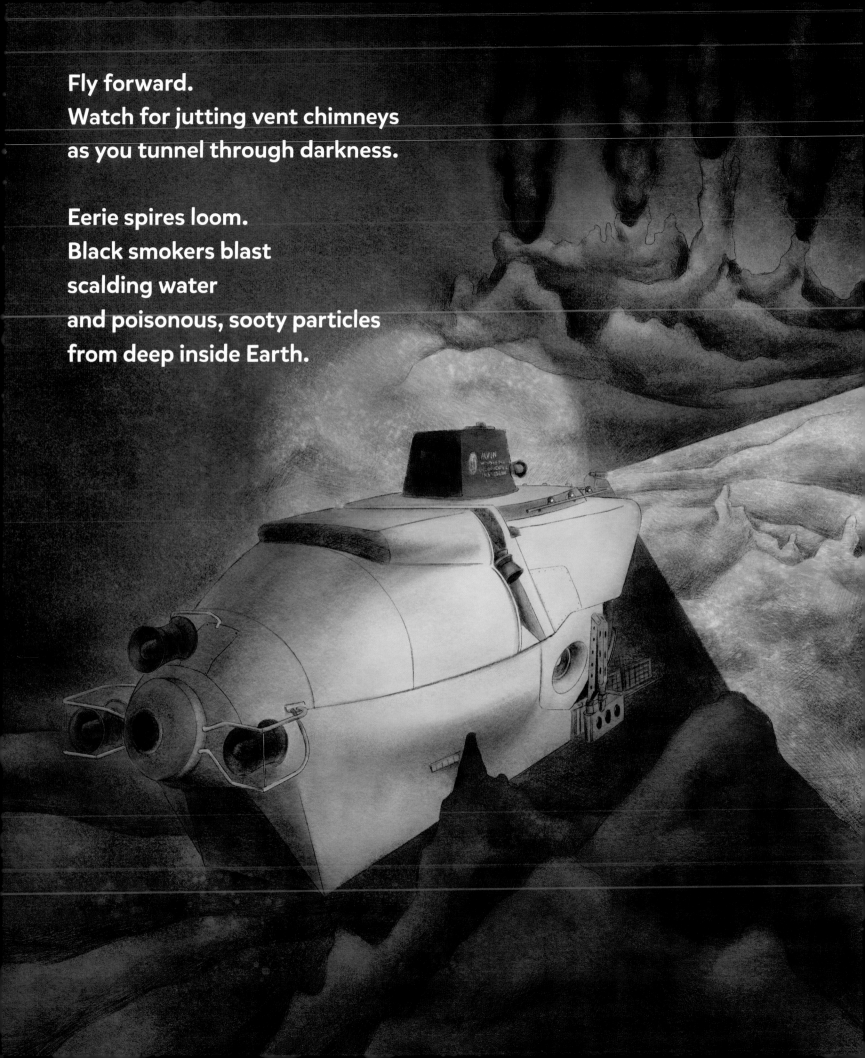

Cottony fields of bacteria
wave in currents.
Shimmering water swirls.
Pompeii worms,
like sausages sporting dreadlocks,
move in and out of tubes.
Dinner-plate-sized clams
nestle among rocks.
Giant tube worms'
feathery plumes sway.

Few humans have seen
this blooming oasis.
The vigor and variety
of life is breathtaking.

Noon

Eat peanut butter and honey sandwiches
while you work.
Don't drink too much.
No toilet on board.

Orange flashes outside.
An unexpected visitor
wraps pudgy arms
around *Alvin*'s manipulator arm.
Tilt and zoom a video camera
on the Dumbo octopus.
Record its investigation
before it slips away.

Animals here thrive
in toxic chemicals,
blistering temperatures,
and intense pressure.
But you're safe inside *Alvin*.

You're tired
yet energized
as you hunch over the controls.
You're a pioneer of the deep.

2:00 p.m.
An elusive eelpout
winds among tube worms.
Press the joystick left
to shift *Alvin* sideways.
Be careful!
Rocky columns
could collapse
and pin you
two miles
below the surface.

Lock the manipulator arm into place.
Toggle the slurp gun into position
and creep *Alvin* forward,
ready to suction the fish—*slurp*!

Scientists cheer your capture.

:00 p.m.

ttery's low.

me to go.

all surface controller:

REQUEST PERMISSION TO SURFACE."

CLEARED TO SURFACE."

Drop port weight—
click, shhhh.
Alvin rolls slightly again,
then slowly rises

UP UP UP

through midnight darkness
and starry bioluminescence.

Inky blackness
lightens to deep blue-green.

UP UP UP.

Blue-green brightens to aqua.

UP UP UP.

Aqua becomes clear.

Alvin breaks the surface.

"KAQP *ATLANTIS*, THIS IS *ALVIN*, CHANNEL 72."

"WE GOT YOU LOUD AND CLEAR."

Await divers

to assist your return to *Atlantis*.

5:00 p.m.
Mission accomplished!
Stand,
stretch stiff legs,
and breathe salty air.
Squint as eyes adjust
to glaring sunlight.
Smile at the crew
crowded on deck,
eager
to examine
your discoveries.

The Story Behind Flying Deep

When I was teaching fourth grade, Don Collasius, a former *Alvin* pilot, visited my classroom. My students and I were fascinated by his stories about giant tube worms, black smokers spewing toxic hot water, and fish that explode when brought to the surface. We enjoyed learning insider details such as how *Alvin*'s pilot and passengers go to the bathroom (in a bottle called a HERE: Human Element Range Extender), and that a sign on board Research Vessel (R/V) *Atlantis* reminds passengers to "PB4UGO."

I was hooked, and the seeds of this book were planted.

I set this story at a place called Nine North, 550 miles off the coast of Acapulco, Mexico. Scientists have tracked the ebb and flow of life at Nine North through more than one cycle of a destructive volcanic eruption and rebirth. It is a place where constant destruction and creation happens. The landscape and life there is constantly changing.

In school, you may have learned that food chains are the building blocks of the food web, and that all food chains begin with the sun. People often think of this as fact. But when scientists discovered hydrothermal vents, they found food chains that exist far from the sun's rays. They learned that chemicals blasted from deep inside Earth are converted to food by microbes and bacteria, which are then eaten by animals living near the vents.

I completed extensive research to write this book. I read a lot about *Alvin* and *Alvin* pilots. I scoured the Woods

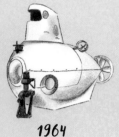
1964

1968

1970

Hole Oceanographic Institution (WHOI) and the National Oceanic and Atmospheric Administration (NOAA) websites for details regarding *Alvin*, pilots, and hydrothermal vents. Once I had a solid working knowledge, I turned to an expert. I spent time with Don Collasius, talking about his experiences as an *Alvin* pilot. He told me stories about glowing deep-sea organisms, a purple octopus as tall as a man, and a shark that nearly attacked a swimmer assisting with an *Alvin* launch.

I visited the WHOI Ocean Science Exhibit Center and the communications office, where I met Joanne Tromp, WHOI communications director. Joanne shared publications that informed my research, and she connected me to Bruce Strickrott, a current *Alvin* pilot and the manager of the *Alvin* Group at WHOI.

Bruce's help was invaluable. When we met, I climbed inside *Alvin* to experience the tight space and hear the sounds a pilot would hear. We have since shared many follow-up calls and emails as I clarified details. Bruce's humor and passion for his work came through in every exchange. Among the many skills an *Alvin* pilot needs is a sense of humor. Bruce was quoted in a magazine once saying, "The technical skills are obvious, but without humor down there, we're doomed."

Would you like to pilot *Alvin* someday? Since *Alvin* was first launched in 1965, only forty men and one woman have been pilots. But imagine this: you could make a discovery that changes our understanding of the world or of the universe.—*Michelle Cusolito*

Illustrator's Note

In another life, if I had not studied art and spent my career creating books for children, I would have liked to have been a scientist. The two fields aren't that different, I think. I start creating an illustration by making observations and recording what I see, like a scientist. I interpret those observations, and I experiment to see what works best—in this case, to help tell the story in a way that's accurate, engaging, and fun.

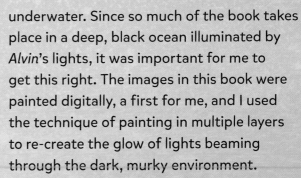

1977

For an artist, the ocean is an amazing playground to explore. It's like an alien world, with animals and life cycles so bizarre they almost seem like imaginary creatures. I wanted to capture some of that sense of wonder for these illustrations, so part of my research involved taking my four-year-old daughter to the New England Aquarium in Boston to see how she reacted to some of the amazing animals on display.

Seeing habitats up close was also helpful to understanding how light functions

1984

underwater. Since so much of the book takes place in a deep, black ocean illuminated by *Alvin*'s lights, it was important for me to get this right. The images in this book were painted digitally, a first for me, and I used the technique of painting in multiple layers to re-create the glow of lights beaming through the dark, murky environment.

I studied dozens of photos and videos of *Alvin* from every angle to understand how the vehicle moves and how its scientific instruments operate. I live close enough to Woods Hole, Massachusetts, to visit *Alvin* in person, but it was out on assignment while I was illustrating this book. So I followed its progress live on social media as *Alvin* explored the Pacific Ocean off the coast of Central America. I also tuned in to see live video of scientists conducting underwater expeditions, which was the closest thing to actually being inside on a trip below the surface.—*Nicole Wong*

1989

ALVIN Facts

- *Alvin* is able to go as deep as 14,764 feet (4,500 meters). That's almost three miles down!
- The titanium wall of *Alvin's* sphere is almost 3 inches thick.
- Inside is close to 7 feet wide (diameter). A tight fit!
- *Alvin* uses iron weights as ballast to help keep it stable. Weight is released at depth, allowing *Alvin* to hover. Weight is also released to return to the surface. The iron left in the ocean degrades over time.

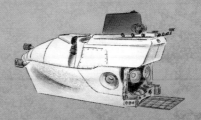

2013

Glossary

Abyss: A deep or seemingly bottomless place.

Bioluminescence: The natural creation of light by some living organisms.

Black smoker: A kind of hydrothermal vent that spews black particles that look like smoke from a chimney.

Carbon dioxide scrubber: A machine that removes carbon dioxide from inside *Alvin*. (Humans exhale carbon dioxide. Too much of it inside *Alvin* is dangerous to the passengers.)

Ecosystem: A community where organisms interact with and depend on each other and their environment.

Hydrothermal vent: An opening on the seafloor that spews hot water, chemicals, and minerals. Minerals build up to form chimney-shaped vents located on the seafloor in volcanically active places (such as where tectonic plates meet).

Launch coordinator: A person on board Research Vessel (R/V) *Atlantis* who coordinates the launch and recovery of *Alvin*.

Oxygen: An element humans need in gas form to survive.

Surface controller: A licensed *Alvin* pilot who oversees all aspects of the dive from the bridge of *R/V Atlantis*.

Underwater volcano: Like volcanoes on land, these form where Earth's crust is thin. An eruption causes gas, ash, or lava to rupture Earth's surface. Hot lava blasted into the ocean can kill plants and animals.

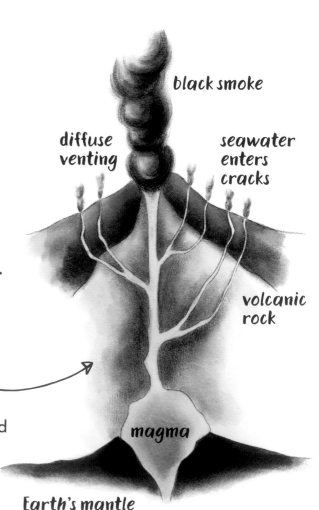

black smoke

diffuse venting

seawater enters cracks

volcanic rock

magma

Earth's mantle

Organisms in Flying Deep

Bacteria: Tiny organisms that can only be seen with a microscope. Near hydrothermal vents, bacteria convert chemical energy from deep inside Earth into food that sustains life.

Dumbo octopus: An octopus with two large fins that resemble the ears of Disney's Dumbo elephant. Dumbo octopuses live in the deepest, most extreme parts of the ocean.

Eelpout: A general name for a group of 250 species of eel-like fish that thrive in extreme environments.

Ghost crabs: Small white crabs that are common near hydrothermal vents.

Giant clams: Large clams (up to a foot across) that live near hydrothermal vents. They smell like rotten eggs because of sulfur in the water near vents.

Giant tube worms: Up to six feet long, these animals live inside tubes at hydrothermal vents. Their bright-red plumes are full of hemoglobin, the same protein found in human blood.

Pompeii worms: These small tube worms (four or five inches long) live on the sides of hydrothermal vents. Unlike giant tube worms, Pompeii worms can move in and out of their tubes.

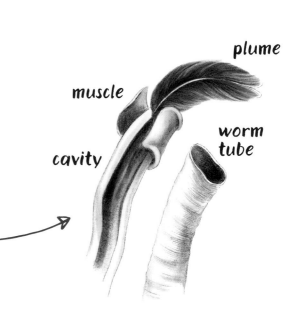

plume

muscle

cavity

worm tube

Learn more

Books

Berne, Jennifer, and Éric Puybaret. *Manfish: A Story of Jacques Cousteau.*
 San Francisco: Chronicle, 2008.

Jenkins, Steve. *Down, Down, Down: A Journey to the Bottom of the Sea.* Boston:
 Houghton Mifflin Harcourt, 2009.

Nivola, Claire A. *Life in the Ocean: The Story of Oceanographer Sylvia Earle.* New York: Farrar
 Straus Giroux, 2012.

Yaccarino, Dan. *The Fantastic Undersea Life of Jacques Cousteau.* New York: Alfred A. Knopf, 2009.

Film

Volcanoes of the Deep Sea, directed by Stephen Low (Dorval, Quebec: The Stephen Low
 Company, 2003).
 A film for all ages featuring stunning images.

Websites

Main Page for *Alvin*, Woods Hole Oceanographic Institution
 www.whoi.edu/main/hov-alvin
 Overview of *Alvin*'s history with information about *Alvin*'s recent upgrade and videos.

Dive Deeper in *Alvin*, Woods Hole Oceanographic Institution Vimeo Channel
 https://vimeo.com/album/4261384
 Nine videos provide information about *Alvin* and the work of the scientists who dive in *Alvin*.

Sea Vent Viewer, National Science Foundation
 www.nsf.gov/news/overviews/earth-environ/interactive.jsp
 Interactive website where students can learn more about *Alvin* and deep-sea vents.

Volcanoes of the Deep Sea, The Stephen Low Company
 www.stephenlow.com/project/volcanoes-of-the-deep-sea
 Includes a downloadable teacher's guide with activities.

Author's Pinterest board

www.pinterest.com/mcusolito/flying-deep/
 Additional resources, including films, children's books, and adult books used to research
 Flying Deep.

The URLs listed here were accurate at publication, but websites often change. If a URL doesn't work,
you can use the internet to find more information.